The City of London in retreat

The EU's attack on Britain's most successful industry

Professor Tim Congdon

The Bruges Group

First Published 2014
by The Bruges Group,
214 Linen Hall, 162-168 Regent Street, London W1B 5TB

Copyright © The Bruges Group 2014
http://www.brugesgroup.com/
www.brugesgroup.com
Bruges Group publications are not intended to represent a
corporate view of European and international developments.
Contributions are chosen on the basis of their intellectual
rigour and their ability to open up new avenues for debate.

Bretwalda Books
Unit 8, Fir Tree Close, Epsom,
Surrey KT17 3LD
info@BretwaldaBooks.com

ISBN 978-1-910440-03-2

Main points of Tim Congdon's
The City of London in retreat

1. The UK's international financial services sector (i.e., "the City of London") was by far the most dynamic part of the UK economy from the 1960s to 2008. The City remains massively important to London's prosperity and indeed to the economic well-being of the UK as a whole. Unhappily, the City of London is now in retreat, with excessive and unfriendly EU regulation being largely to blame.

2. In the fourth quarter of 2013 business services accounted for 1,517,000 jobs in London, which was 28.0% of all London employment. (Their proportion in UK employment as a whole was much lower, 15.7%.)

3. London-based international business services (i.e., *both* financial *and* non-financial services) employ about 5% of the UK's working population and produce perhaps 8% - 10% of its national output, with most of that output exported. Continued growth of these activities at above the growth rate of output as a whole would be positive for the UK's *average* living standards.

4. The UK's position as a world leader in the provision of international business services is under threat. A move of regulation from the UK to EU institutions is under way as a result of the Lisbon Treaty. The UK's financial services industries have increasingly been subject to harmful and unsympathetic regulatory interventions from the EU, and the extra regulatory burden is an important reason for the halt to growth. The rapid growth in the UK's financial services industry in the 40 years to 2008 now lies in the past. EU-level regulation is more costly, cumbersome and inefficient than the previous regulatory structure under the UK's own control.

5. The regulatory powers of the EU bureaucracies are determined by qualified majority voting in the EU's Council of Ministers. The UK has no veto. This is one reason, although only one reason, why a radical re-appraisal of EU membership has become essential.

Contents

The Author

Professor Tim Congdon is one of the Britain's leading economic commentators. His most prominent public role was as a member of the Treasury Panel of Independent Forecasters (the so-called "wise men") between 1992 and 1997, which advised the Chancellor of the Exchequer on economic policy. In 1989 he founded Lombard Street Research, one of the City of London's leading economic consultancies, and was its managing director until 2001.

He left the City in 2005 in order to have more time to write. But the financial crisis caused him to return to investment and economic consultancy, and in 2009 he set up another research business, International Monetary Research Ltd. His latest venture is the establishment of a new Institute of International Monetary Research in association with the University of Buckingham. The institute will monitor trends in money and banking around the world. As well as advising companies and financial institutions on the wider macroeconomic impact of monetary developments, it will sponsor academic research, publish research documents, and contribute to the public debate on economic policy issues.

Professor Congdon was an honorary professor at Cardiff Business School from 1990–2006 and a visiting professor at Cass Business School from 1998–2004. He has written a number of books on monetary policy, contributes widely to the financial press, and makes frequent radio and television appearances. He was awarded the CBE for services to economic debate in 1997.

Professor Congdon is also the author of the Bruges Group paper, *Will the EU's Constitution Rescue its Currency?* Professor Congdon is a member of the Bruges Group's Academic Advisory Council.

Executive Summary

How is Britain to remain a well-paid, successful and influential nation in the 21st century?

In our own nation such service activities as financial services, legal work, accountancy, publishing, journalism, business information, management consultancy and advertising (plus its associated activities of design and market research) tend to be located in London and to be well-paid by UK standards. Much of the output of these industries is exported. Left to themselves, current pay differentials argue that the UK is likely to specialize in these areas, which might be termed "international business services".

In the fourth quarter of 2013 business services accounted for 1,517,000 jobs in London, which was 28.0% of all London employment. (Their proportion in UK employment as a whole was 15.7%). Much of the wealth creation derives from the financial services industry, which until 2008 was by far the most dynamic sector of the UK economy.

London-based international business services (i.e., *both* financial *and* non-financial services) employ about 5% of the UK's working population and produce perhaps 8% – 10% of its national output, with most of that output exported. Continued growth of these activities at above the growth rate of output as a whole would be positive for the UK's *average* living standards.

In 1991 the UK's exports of international business services were £18.7 billion and its imports were £6.3 billion; in 2008 the corresponding figures were £126 billion and £48.9 billion. Exports of these services had grown at a compound annual rate of 12.7%. In 2008 the surplus was no less than £77.2 billion. The bulk of the value added in London-based financial services is sold to the rest of the world. These exports are vital in paying for the UK's imports.

In the 17 years to 2008 growth of the UK's financial services exports was faster than that of its business services exports overall. As exports of financial services were £6.4 billion in 1991, the compound annual rate of growth to 2008 was a remarkable 12.9%

a year. But this growth came to an abrupt halt in 2008. From 2008 to 2013 exports of international business services continued to grow, if at just 2.2% a year, but exports of financial services by themselves fell.

However, the UK's position as a world leader in the provision of international business services is under threat. The move of regulation from the UK to EU institutions is an important reason for the halt to growth. The UK's financial services industries have increasingly been subject to harmful and unsympathetic regulatory interventions from the EU. The rapid growth in the UK's financial services industry in the 40 years to 2008 now lies in the past. EU-level regulation is more costly, cumbersome and inefficient than the previous regulatory structure under the UK's own control.

The Lisbon Treaty allowed the European Commission to impose a new regulatory blueprint on the financial sector, including the City of London's unique and specialist activities. The Commission proposed a "European Systemic Risk Council" and a "European System of Financial Supervisors". The ESFS is now embodied in three newly-created institutions, all with full "legal personality", the European Banking Authority, the European Insurance and Occupational Pensions Authority, and the European Securities Authority. These authorities can override the national authorities, including those set up for the UK by the British government and empowered by legislation from our own Parliament.

The job of the EBA, the EIOPA and the ESA is to forge a common set of rules, which is to apply uniformly and consistently across EU member states. Under the ESFS umbrella (i.e., that of the European Commission ultimately), they are to resolve disputes between national supervisors and regulators, and work towards "a common regulatory culture". In the extreme they have the power to close down a British financial institution. The EU bureaucracy has already interfered extensively, and on numerous occasions, in the management of UK financial institutions.

Let it be emphasized that the exact powers of the three ESFS bureaucracies are determined by qualified majority voting in the EU's Council of Ministers. The UK has no veto. This is one reason, although only one reason, why a radical re-appraisal of EU membership has become essential.

Introduction: another look, five years later

On 26th October 2009 I gave a talk to the Bruges Group about financial regulation and the City of London. My themes were two-fold,

- that the Lisbon Treaty would lead to the transfer of financial regulation from the British state and its agencies (including the Bank of England and the then Financial Services Authority) to European Union institutions which would be under the umbrella of the European Commission, and

- that this transfer of regulation would disadvantage "the City of London", understood as the UK's international financial services industries plus the headquarters operations of UK financial businesses.

The Bruges Group recorded the talk, and I was able quite quickly to edit the transcript and put together a pamphlet with the title *The City of London under Threat: the EU and its attack on Britain's most successful industry*. The Lisbon Treaty undoubtedly did mean that financial regulation would become an EU 'competence' and that the powers of the UK's own regulatory authorities would be reduced at the expense of newly-formed EU bodies.

Nevertheless, the treaty was a complex document that was not easy to summarize in either a press release or a newspaper headline. A huge change in what one might term "the constitutional arrangements" for UK finance was in prospect, but media coverage was negligible. It is clear (see pages 17 – 18) that key UK policy-makers had not understood or anticipated the implications of the Lisbon Treaty for their own powers and responsibilities. These policy-makers might be described as badly informed, but that would misrepresent and understate the problem. The truth was many of them simply had not been informed at all. The actual transfer of regulatory competence was by means of a "Communication" from the European Commission, not a new statute from the UK's own legislature. To the best of my knowledge, the Communication – which began life with a proposal from the Commission on 23rd September 2009 – was not reported in detail by any British newspaper at the time. At any rate, by early 2011 three new EU-level supervisory authorities had been created. (The subject is discussed on page 16). Whether the British government liked this development or not, the new authorities had the task of establishing an EU-wide supervisory framework. Crucially, they could override national regulatory bodies.

The current essay is an update, five years later, of the consequences of the regulatory upheaval for the City of London. The central messages are simple, that

- the rapid growth in the UK's financial services industry in the 40 years to 2008 lies in the past, and

- a major reason for this setback is that EU-level regulation is more costly, cumbersome and inefficient than the previous regulatory structure under the UK's own control.

The essay has therefore been given the title *The City of London in Retreat: the EU's attack on Britain's most successful industry*. Surprisingly, opinion surveys show that many people working in the UK financial sector want the UK to remain in the EU. Well, it cannot be overlooked that the UK's financial services exports are lower than in 2008, and that the City of London has started to slip in league tables ranking international financial centres.

As in 2009, I am grateful to the Bruges Group for publishing this pamphlet. Will I return to this subject another five years from now, in 2019? Perhaps. I hope that my analysis proves to have been wrong. Very sincerely, I will be pleased if the next five years sees a resumption of the spectacular growth that the City's industries enjoyed before regulatory control was moved from London to other European cities. Let me make clear that I nevertheless expect to be proved right.

The City of London in retreat:
the EU's attack on Britain's most successful industry

Regulatory challenges to the prosperity of the City of London and, by extension, to the London and UK economies, have become increasingly serious in recent years. The argument of this essay is that most such challenges now arise from the UK's membership of the European Union or at least have an important EU dimension to them. The essay is an update of an exercise almost five years ago in November 2009, based on a talk a few weeks earlier to the Bruges Group. In 2009 much of the discussion was about the threat to the City of London which EU policy might eventually represent; today the concern must instead be about the harm which EU policy has already done, as well as the prospect of even greater damage in the future. Much of the trouble stems from the Lisbon Treaty, which received its final approval from EU governments and parliaments just as the first version of this essay was being published.

The essay works on an assumption which might seem so obvious as hardly to require statement. This is that, as a sovereign nation, Britain has a government which determines public policy to benefit its citizens. More generally, British public policy should promote Britain's way of life and living standards. This may seem banal, but in modern Europe the notion of "sovereign nations" and national interest are being challenged.[1] One aim of the essay is to position the UK's current economic challenge – to remain a rich, successful and influential nation in the 21st century – in a larger historical context. In the 25 years to the Great Recession trends in the structure of the economy suggest that the British people were making a good response to that challenge. Unfortunately, this response has increasingly been subject to a variety of harmful and unsympathetic interventions from the EU, as well as from other

---

[1] Some academic openly support "cosmopolitanism", understood as "a concern with the equal moral status of each and every human being" which creates "a bedrock of interest in what it is that human beings have in common, independently of their particular familial, ethical, national and religious affiliations". (This is a quotation from p. x of David Held *Cosmopolitanism* [London: Polity, 2010]. Professor Held is currently Master of University College, Durham. He has advocated what he terms "cosmopolitan democracy", to be contrasted with democracy at the level of the nation state.)

international regulatory initiatives. These interventions and initiatives have gained momentum during and since the Great Recession.

The economic challenge of the early 21st century

Britain was the pioneer of the industrial revolution, in which factory-based production and employment superseded earlier types of production in farms and workshops. The debate about the UK's economic future continues to reflect nostalgia for its initial leadership in factory-based activity. A 2009 collection of papers from the Civitas think-tank *Nations Choose Prosperity* advocated an explicit "industrial policy".[2] More recently, John Mills has published a pamphlet *There Is An alternative*, also under the Civitas logo, asserting that manufacturing has "our main capacity for paying our way in the world". It urged a "rebalancing" of the economy towards manufacturing industry so that the UK economy can remain "capable of keeping up with the rest of the world".[3]

In fact, several types of value creation coexisted inside the factories of the industrial revolution. Routine, repetitive and structured tasks, which led to the mass manufacture of more or less identical tangible products, typically took place on the "shop floor". But factories also included other floors or slightly separate buildings, where each item of work was more individual and unpredictable, and required the exercise of judgement, responsibility and intelligence. The tasks included the design, marketing and sale of products, the organization of finance and payments, the handling of legal and other disputes, and most important of all the overarching management function of integrating factors of production. These tasks were for "the bosses" or, in the vernacular, "the gaffers". Of course, the bosses' work was more intellectually demanding, more interesting and better-paid than that of the shop-floor workers.

The industrial revolution began in Britain in the middle of the 18th century. Crucial to its success was the specialisation celebrated in Adam Smith's 1776 *Wealth of Nations*. As is well-known, the *Wealth of Nations* argued that free trade would cause people and companies to concentrate on lines of production where they had an advantage,

---

[2]   Ruth Lea (ed.) *Nations Choose Prosperity: why Britain needs an industrial policy* (London: Civitas, 2009).

[3]   John Mills *There Is An Alternative* (London: Civitas, 2014), p. vii and p. 5.

to sell the resulting outputs abroad and to buy from other countries products where these countries were particularly efficient. Industrialisation and specialisation have now spread across the globe, embracing even such huge nations as the formerly inward-looking and backward China and India. Whereas in the middle of the 19th century, the UK came first in a wide range of industries, including such iconic items as cotton and woollen goods, iron and coal, today there are hardly any traditional industrial activities in which it is a leader. With a mere 1 per cent of the world's population, that is hardly surprising.

How, then, is Britain to remain a well-paid, successful and influential nation in the new context? A reasonable answer is that we should try to do the well-paid work, the bosses' work, the kind of work that was not on the factory shop-floor in the early era of industrialization. We need to specialise not on routine and repetitive types of production, dependent on low-level or medium-level technologies which are widely known and easily copied. As far as possible, we want people in the rest of the world to be doing the low-skill work in factories, mines and plantations, whereas we should be doing the complex tasks, the sort of work that could not be done on the shop floor because it was too difficult and required exceptional talents. Of course, individuals are the best judges of their own destiny, and they must decide for themselves where their abilities and skills can be best employed. Nevertheless, current pay differentials in our own nation argue that we should be concentrating on such activities as financial services, marketing, design, advertising, legal work, accountancy, publishing, journalism, business information, the arts (music, drama, criticism, and the creation of a range of associated artefacts) and the various forms of management consultancy. We should also want the UK to be the headquarters centre for companies with production facilities across the globe.

These are the kinds of production where the challenge varies from day to day, the response has to be personal and sometimes original and unique, and high-level skills, initiative and flair are called into play. They need people who can think hard, exercise judgement, take responsibility and demonstrate creativity. If Britain is to be rich in coming decades, if it is to enjoy the economic future that might be expected from its rather special past, its people need to focus on high-value-added brain-work, not in the low-value-added making of things with our hands (which is the literal meaning of the word "manufacture"). Of course the markets for high-value-added brain-work – like the markets for mass-produced manufactures – are global. Logically, if Britain is to be a prosperous country by world standards in the 21st century, it will specialize in a range of activities that might be called "international business services". [4]

(Let me state here – to avoid misunderstanding – that in the framing of public policy I am neither for nor against manufacturing, and neither for nor against services. Some manufacturing processes are complex, individual, unique and so on, and require brain as well as brawn. I believe that, as far as possible, public policy should be neutral in its attitude towards different economic activities. I also believe that – on the whole – exports of business services are likely to generate higher valued added per person in the UK than exports of bob-basic manufactured goods. The important thing is to give people and companies the freedom to select the most profitable outlets for their energies and resources.)

Britain's recent pattern of specialisation

The British are notorious for self-denigration.[5] It may therefore come as a surprise to see how far, in the decades leading up to the Great Recession and the 2009 Lisbon Treaty, their nation's pattern of specialisation was moving in the direction endorsed by the discussion so far. More recently much has gone wrong.

We need first to assess the UK economy in the global setting. How big is the UK's economy compared with the world's? Although the precise figure depends on the statistical conventions adopted, the UK at present accounts for about 3% of world output. The UK share of world output fell precipitously after the Second World War, but it was more stable in the 25 years from the early 1980s. The decline continued, but it was gentler than in the previous 25 years. However, since the mid-Noughties the decline in the UK's relative economic importance has accelerated, as shown by Chart 1. By 2018 the International Monetary Fund expects that the UK will account for about 2.5% of total world output.

Has the UK been concentrating on international business services, in line with the pattern of specialisation proposed here? It turns out that – in the 25 years to the mid-Noughties, the period in which our share of world output did not change much – that is exactly what we were doing. Chart 2 shows the UK's exports and imports of international business services since 1991, when the figures were first prepared in their current form and published in the annual *Pink Book* of UK balance-of-payments statistics.[6] In 1991 the UK's exports of international business services were £18.7

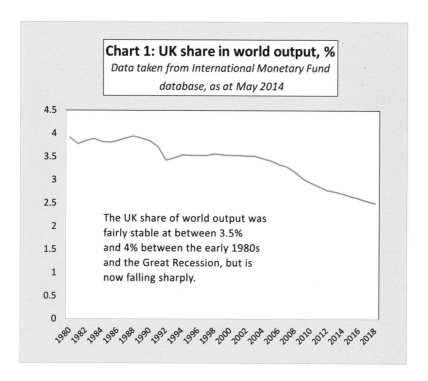

Chart 1: UK share in world output, %
Data taken from International Monetary Fund database, as at May 2014

The UK share of world output was fairly stable at between 3.5% and 4% between the early 1980s and the Great Recession, but is now falling sharply.

billion and its imports were £6.3 billion; in 2008 the corresponding figures were £126 billion and £48.9 billion. Exports of these services had grown at a compound annual rate of 12.7% and imports of 12.9%. Because exports were and remain so much larger than imports, the UK's surplus on this type of international trade widened despite the very slightly faster growth rate of imports. In 2008 the surplus was no less than £77.2 billion.

---

4   Where do "international business services" begin and end? I have been guided by the data produced by the Office for National Statistics, with the categories devised by the official statisticians. One result is that international tourism and travel revenues, including – for example – foreigners' payments for UK hotel and restaurants are excluded. The industries inside my "international business services" are those represented in Chart 2. No dividing line is perfect.

5   "Surely then, we British ought to feel more self-confident. One of the reasons that we do not is that we have developed the habit of continually running ourselves down." Clive Aslet *Anyone for England?: a search for British identity* (London: Little, Brown and Company, 1997), p. 240.

6   Office for National Statistics (Derek Vere [ed.]) *United Kingdom Balance of Payments: Pink Book* (Newport: ONS, 2009).

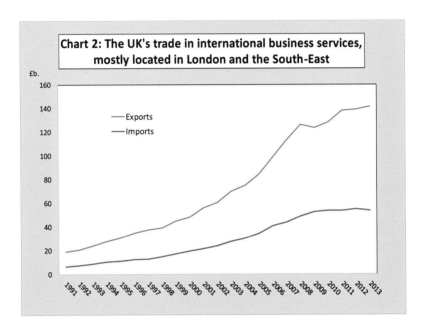

Chart 2: The UK's trade in international business services, mostly located in London and the South-East

These were encouraging numbers. Over the same 17-year period the UK's national output (which appears in the national accounts as "gross value added") advanced in money terms from £542.4 billion to £1,312.1 billion, which gives a compound annual rate of increase of 5.3%. Whereas exports of international business services were 3.4% of national output in 1991, they were 9.6% of national output in 2008. Clearly, the UK's involvement in international business services had come to represent a much increased share of its total production. These are the types of activity that, according to the argument here, require judgement, flair and individual responsibility, and are correspondingly well-paid. This is where Britain's people had been concentrating their skills, talents and capital. The evidence was that companies and individuals wanted to move into a "post-industrial era", in the sense that standardized manufacturing activities would leave the UK and high-value-added, high-income business services would take their place.

Now let us update the figures to 2013. It is already obvious from Chart 2 that the boom in international business services faltered in 2008. Exports and imports have grown in the last five years, but at a much weaker pace than before. The table below gives precise figures. The compound annual rate of increase in exports of international business services was a mere 2.2% in the five years to 2013, very feeble compared with the previous 17 years. These exports rose more or less in line with money GDP, but were outpaced by the majority of the UK's exports, which went up by 3.3% a year. The new weakness of business service exports is noteworthy, because a big devaluation in 2008 ought to have given them extra stimulus. On the face of it, something has gone wrong in this part of the UK economy compared with the two decades up to 2008.

International business services in the UK growth pattern, 1991 - 2013		
	1991 - 2008	2008 - 2013
Exports of international business services	12.7%	2.2%
Imports of international business services	12.9%	1.8%
Total exports of goods and services	6.7%	3.3%
Total imports of goods and services	7.2%	2.9%
Money GDP	5.3%	2.0%

Calculated from annual data; all numbers are in money terms, they are *not* in constant prices.
Source: Office for National Statistics

Financial services within the overall pattern of specialisation

The phrase "international business services" is useful in understanding an important trend towards specialisation in the UK economy in the last three decades, but a multitude of smaller specialisations are embraced within it. The pie in Chart 3 shows the relative size in 2008 of the various "industries" within the larger group. Exports of financial services totalled £54.8 billion and constituted getting on for half (43.5%) the total of £126 billion. So-called "other business services" – legal work, medical work, accountancy, advertising, consultancy and so on – were the next category, with £43.6 billion or 34.6% of the total. Insurance exports – largely consisting of "unearned" premiums – were £13.2 billion, although the figure is complicated by reinsurance payments between UK and foreign insurers.[7] Smaller categories were

---

[7] The measurement of the "insurance" items in international payments statistics is extraordinarily difficult. I understand that – to keep matters simple – the official statisticians often take cash flow numbers, as anything else is too problematic. So the insurance numbers in the text here do not correspond to the usual economic understanding of "value added" and are not on a national accounts basis.

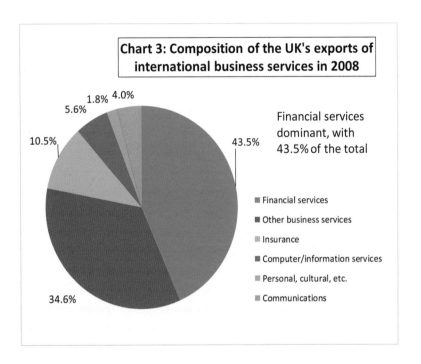

Chart 3: Composition of the UK's exports of international business services in 2008

Financial services dominant, with 43.5% of the total

43.5%

- Financial services
- Other business services
- Insurance
- Computer/information services
- Personal, cultural, etc.
- Communications

4.0%
1.8%
5.6%
10.5%
34.6%

"communications" (mostly the overseas receipts of the UK's telecommunications companies) of £5.1 billion, and "personal and cultural" of £2.2billion. (The "personal and cultural" category would include, for example, the overseas income of British orchestras and pop stars.)

So – in summary, with insurance included – exports of financial services were about half the total exports of international business services in the year when the Great Recession hit. Further, exports of financial services constituted a remarkable 5% of national output. Without doubt a significant chunk – perhaps at least a half – of this 5% figure came from "the City of London" in the precise geographical sense of the Square Mile. But by 2008 a high proportion of City-type employment was outside the Square Mile, although within London. The Square Mile had simply been too cramped to accommodate all the growth that might have occurred within it. I will revert to this spill-over effect later in the essay.[8]

In the 17 years to 2008 growth of the UK's financial services exports was even faster than that of its business services exports overall. As exports of financial services were

£6.4billion in 1991, the compound annual rate of growth to 2008 was a remarkable 12.9% a year. While there are conceptual problems putting a UK-calculated, sterling-based number on the same basis as world output, there is little question that the growth rate of the UK's financial services activities has been about double that of world output over the last two or three decades. The City's various activities have been a spectacular boom area in an economy that is relatively slow-growing by world standards. Incomes per head in the UK financial sector are much above those in the rest of the economy, reflecting the international demand for its output, and its ability to benefit from globalisation and the information technology revolution. (Financial services are heavy users of computer-based hardware and software, and also of telecommunications.) Surely, a good argument can be made that we should continue to specialize here. Financial services are likely to remain both dynamic and characterised by high-value-added per person throughout the 21st century.

Halt to growth since 2008

As was noted a few paragraphs ago, the UK's exports of business services have grown much more slowly since 2008 than in the preceding few decades. Has there also been a change in the relative importance of different activities within the larger business services total? To answer this question, the following pie chart needs to be compared with the previous one. Some jockeying of position has taken place between the main types of activity. Clearly, financial services as such have declined in relative importance. Whereas in 2008 they were responsible for almost 45% of total UK business service exports, in 2013 that proportion had dropped to a little more than a third.

If insurance were also included, financial service exports last year were about £60 billion, 40% of total business service exports and slightly less than 4% of national output. They remained hugely important to our economy, but had clearly lost ground. The chart shows that "other business services" are now bigger than financial services. The "other business services" category is a bit of a ragbag, but includes such branches of service production as the law, accountancy, management consultancy, advertising, design work and so on. Some people might feel that these rather miscellaneous

---

[8]   I first discussed this spill-over effect in a Lombard Street Research report on *Growth Prospects of City Industries* for the Corporation of London in April 1998. See *Growth Prospects of City Industries* (London: Corporation of London, 1998), pp. 19 – 20.

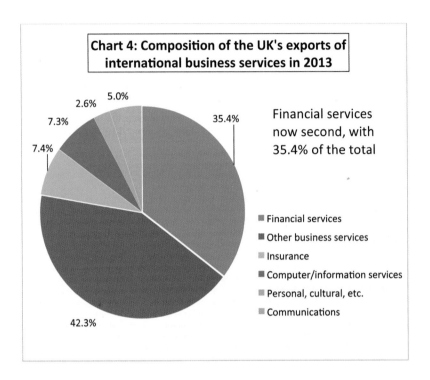

Chart 4: Composition of the UK's exports of international business services in 2013

5.0%
2.6%
7.3%
7.4%
35.4%
42.3%

Financial services now second, with 35.4% of the total

■ Financial services
■ Other business services
▨ Insurance
■ Computer/information services
▨ Personal, cultural, etc.
▨ Communications

activities are more "socially worthwhile" than financial services, but in truth much legal and accounting work is a spin-off from the financial sector. At any rate, the value of the UK's financial services exports dropped by about 10% between 2008 and 2013, whereas its exports of "other business services" made progress, rising from £43.6 billion to £59.7 billion. To the extent that "something went wrong" with the UK's business service exports in the five years to 2013, the data show clearly that the setback was specifically in the financial area.

The message for London's economy

A constant refrain in the recessions of the early 1980s and early 1990s was "where will the jobs come from?" The jeremiahs about the UK's economic performance could not imagine a world of strong employment growth and sharply reduced unemployment. Chart 5 shows the growth rate of employment in London's "business services" industries (as this category is measured in the relevant official statistics) since the

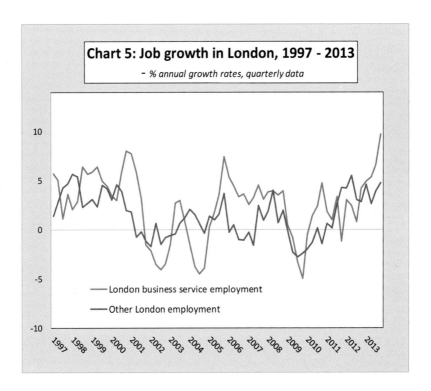

Chart 5: Job growth in London, 1997 - 2013
- % annual growth rates, quarterly data

London business service employment

Other London employment

mid-1990s.[9] The compound annual rate of growth of this kind of employment was 2.5%, but in some years (including, perhaps surprisingly, 2013) the figure was an extraordinary 7% - 9% a year.[10] So we see an obvious link between the boom in the UK's exports of business services and job creation. (Three groups were included in the "business service" total, "finance and insurance", "professional, scientific and

---

[9]   The data used here were obtained from the Nomis database in the Office for National Statistics website. The database gives numbers for employment in various industrial categories in all the UK's local authorities. The industrial categories in the Nomis employment data cannot be matched up precisely with the categories in the official balance-of-payments data. This is a nuisance, but there are limits to what official statisticians can do.

[10] The employment surge in 2013 is a striking feature of the chart. The explanation seems to be that non-financial business services grew very strongly last year. According to a Cities of Opportunity survey by the accountancy and consultancy firm, PwC, London came top in 2013, ahead of New York, Singapore, Toronto and San Francisco. (Harriet Dennys 'London: powerhouse on top of the world', report in *The Daily Telegraph*, 19th May 2014.) To quote the report, "London received top ranking for software and multimedia development and design, [and] finished second overall for broadband quality." While the financial sector is contracting, London is re-inventing itself as a digital media hub.

technical activities", and "information and communication". In the fourth quarter of 2013 they accounted for 1,517,000 jobs in London, which was 28.0% of all London employment. The proportion of the three groups in UK employment was 15.7%.)

The material I am presenting may appear to glorify London, its economy and its pre-eminence as a centre for international business services. Let me reiterate that I am not against manufacturing and would strongly deprecate official policies to discriminate against it. (I would also strongly deprecate policies to discriminate against services.)[11] Similarly, I am of course not "against Britain outside London". However, the truth is that most of the UK's international business service activities are based in London. Anyone talking about the international business services sector in the UK will, inescapably, be talking mostly about the international business services sector in London. But it needs to be emphasized that the whole of the British economy, and not London in isolation, benefits from the dynamism of international business service activities.

First, industries within the "international business services" group are not self-contained and unlinked to the rest of the UK economy. They rely on massive inputs of information technology, with a high resulting demand for software (i.e., people at the end of the day). The programmers and technicians may live in Greater London or they may commute from outside. At any rate, there is a knock-on effect to activities which may be some distance from international business services, purely defined, and from the City of London or the West End in terms of geography.

---

[11]   The 1964 – 70 Labour government imposed a Selective Employment Tax on service industries, in a deliberate attempt to promote manufacturing. The case for the SET was made by the Cambridge economist, Nicholas Kaldor, who showed that the growth of productivity (i.e., output per person) was faster in manufacturing than in services. Kaldor overlooked an obvious possibility that the faster growth of productivity would lead to a cheapening of manufactured products relative to the products of the service industries. In the period under consideration here (i.e., the 1990s and opening years of the 21st century) the UK enjoyed continuous and systematic gains in its international terms of trade. To simplify a complex topic, it charged more for the services it sold to other countries, while the unit value of the exports of these other countries (i.e., our imports, often manufactured in the Far East) declined. Physical measures of productivity can be very misleading as a guide to policy, in a world where relative prices are moving dramatically. In essence, over the last 20 or 30 years the UK's people and companies have taken clever decisions to pull out of industries characterised by rapid growth of physical productivity, because they foresaw that this productivity growth would undermine the industries' ability to maintain prices and increase true value added per person. SET was an administrative nightmare, which was deeply unpopular. It lasted only five years and was scrapped by the Conservative government in 1971. The episode was a warning against official attempts, by means of the tax system, to steer the allocation of resources away from that chosen by private, profit-motivated agents.

Secondly, employment in international business services is mostly in offices. The offices have to be built and maintained, and then refurbished and re-equipped, all of which boosts the regional and national demand for both labour and building materials. The cost of keeping the London office stock in good condition may be of the order of £2 billion - £3 billion a year, resulting in thousands of jobs over and above those in international business services as such. A striking feature of the distribution of office space by borough is that nowadays much of it is outside the traditional locations in the City of London and the City of Westminster. The boom has spread prosperity to other boroughs. If the boom were to continue, that spreading would ultimately be to the UK as a whole.

The final point is that – because of the long boom in these activities, the apparent difficulty of fully meeting the international demand for them and the very high value added per person – incomes in London are well above the national average. While the City of London is exceptional in this respect, even boroughs regarded as relatively poor and downmarket within the London framework are in fact rich by UK standards. What we see here is the spill-over of prosperity in one possibly quite small area (i.e., "the City of London" in the sense of the Square Mile) to neighbouring areas. In practice, if these successful industries are allowed to grow and flourish, the spill-over benefits ought ultimately to spread to the UK as a whole.

In the last few years the media have been furious with bankers for their allegedly excessive bonuses. But do we want to live in a nation with many rich people, who pay a lot of tax and help to cover the cost of the social services and benefits received by the less well-off, or do we want to live in a nation only of poor people? Surely living in a nation with many rich people is better. Roughly speaking, London-based international business services (i.e., *both* financial *and* non-financial services) employ about 5% of the UK's working population and produce perhaps 8% - 10% of its national output, with most of that output exported. Continued growth of these activities at above the growth rate of output as a whole would be positive for the UK's *average* living standards, as more people acquire the skills necessary to participate in high-value-added sectors.

One further comment may be offered on the UK's recent pattern of specialization. No doubt many people resent the high incomes in London's services industries, but these industries have an important merit in the 21st century. They are environmentally far "cleaner" than manufacturing. Let me repeat that I am not against manufacturing.

However, if we have to accept that the modern world is one where public policy will impose penalties on any kind of greenhouse gas and chemical emission, then logically we should concentrate on economic activities that are relatively "green" in their environmental impact. If we want to live in Blake's fabled New Jerusalem, if we want to make our country "a green and pleasant land", it is more sensible to endorse specialisation on international business services than artificially to promote old and dirty manufacturing. (Does it need to be added that the UK's chemicals industry – like that of other European countries – has in any case been undermined by EU environmental legislation, which has resulted in a large-scale transfer of production to the Gulf, and particularly to Saudi Arabia and the United Arab Emirates?)

The need to be able to set the rules

In general, since 1945 international treaties, and the arrangements between nations which reflect those treaties, have tried to be impartial and non-discriminatory. However, all kinds of cross-border trade and finance are subject to rules, laws and regulations, and the blunt truth is that the wording of these rules, laws and regulations affects some nations differently from others. In the various bear gardens of international relations a nation is fortunate if its own views and preferences are major inputs into the rule-making machinery. A great advantage that Britain gained from its empire was that a whole mass of legal principles and regulatory structures across the globe conformed to patterns that were familiar to people who had never left the British Isles. We initially joined the European "construction", then in the form of the Common Market (or the "European Economic Community") back in 1973. At that stage we ceded control over the setting of rules to Brussels in only two areas, external trade (i.e., the common external tariff) and primary production (farming and fisheries). From the early 1970s until the end of the 20th century the regulatory and legal environment for UK financial services continued to be largely a matter for this country. The long and spectacular boom in exports of international financial services began and continued when the UK's own central bank, regulators and legislature were in charge of that environment.

The position today is very different. The Great Financial Crisis of 2008 – 10 would have caused a sharp cyclical reverse for the UK's financial service industries regardless of the particular policies adopted to prevent its recurrence. But matters were made worse by the widespread interpretation of the crisis as originating in a dysfunctional and unsatisfactory banking system. The official response to the crisis, which reflected this interpretation, was two-fold.[12] First, regulation was tightened, with the declared intention of making banks and other financial institutions shrink their operations. Secondly, regulation was shifted from the UK to international bodies of various kinds, but particularly to EU institutions. The transfer of regulatory authority to the EU institutions was largely the result of the Lisbon Treaty. This treaty specified 50 new "competences" (i.e., areas of activity, usually economic activity, subject to official *diktat* of various kinds) in which the Council of Ministers could take decisions by "qualified majority voting". The expansion of EU competences included new responsibilities and powers for financial regulation.

The precise meaning of the EU notion of a "competence" is tricky and needs amplification. In an area where the EU is "competent", an individual nation cannot block "legislation" (i.e., directives and regulations) emanating from the EU, no matter how much it dislikes that legislation or deems the legislation contrary to its own national interest. (To remind, such legislation is typically initiated by the European Commission, agreed in the Council of Ministers and then processed by the European Parliament.) Clearly, in the sphere of activity defined by the 50 new competences the UK cannot set the rules. It cannot set the rules, even though in many cases new rules, laws and regulations will be relevant to the international financial services in which the UK has traditionally been so successful.

How dangerous for the City of London, and the UK's financial services sector more generally, is the situation that has now emerged? In 2009, in accordance with a so-called "Communication from the Commission" giving effect to the terms of the Lisbon Treaty, two new bodies – a European Systemic Risk Council and a European System of Financial Supervisors – were proposed. The ESFS was to be embodied in three new institutions, all of which were to have "legal personality". These were the European Banking Authority, the European Insurance and Occupational Pensions Authority, and the European Securities Authority. The three institutions now exist, and have buildings, staff and organizational infrastructure as well as legal personality. They are located respectively in London, Frankfurt and Paris, even though London is a far larger centre for life insurance and pension fund management than Frankfurt, and has much bigger and more vibrant capital markets than Paris.

---

[12]   I discuss and criticise the standard interpretation of the crisis in Tim Congdon 'What were the causes of the Great Recession?: the mainstream approach vs the monetary interpretation', pp. 1 – 32, *World Economics*, vol. 15 (2), 2014.

The job of the EBA, the EIOPA and the ESA is to forge a common set of rules, which is to apply uniformly and consistently across EU member states. Under the ESFS umbrella (i.e., that of the European Commission ultimately) they are to resolve disputes between national supervisors and regulators, and work towards "a common regulatory culture".[13] Their powers also apply to particular companies and businesses that have pan-European reach, since these are to be not just supervised, but also authorised by an ESFS body. Such companies include credit rating agencies and clearing houses.

Let it be emphasized that the exact powers of the three ESFS bureaucracies are determined by qualified majority voting, so that the UK has no veto. Disputes about the location of regulatory authority – in other words, disputes between national and EU authorities about the definition of "turf" – are to be decided by the European Court of Justice, which has a long record of expanding EU power at the expense of national governments. According to the proposals, if the Commission considers that a national supervisory authority is not compliant with guidelines, an ESFS body may adopt an individual decision addressed to an offending financial institution to require "necessary" action. Such action could include strict compliance under community law, to the point that a particular organization – a bank, an insurance company or whatever – might be closed down. More specifically, if the European Banking Authority disapproves of conduct by – say – Barclays Bank, it could close it down, regardless of the views of the UK's own regulatory authorities. (Some years back I was sent a private e-mail by a German economics professor, which says that the European Commission had been responding here to "suggestions" from the French government. Indeed, public statements were made at the time by French ministers that were blatant in their hostility to the City of London, even though they also betrayed an obvious wish for the wealth and employment associated with international financial services to relocate to Paris.[14])

The UK has suffered an undoubted encroachment on its sovereignty. The power to authorize financial institutions, or to withdraw authorization, has passed from the UK to the EU. Our country has lost this power even if the financial institutions under consideration have mostly UK owners and operate predominantly in the UK. It would be difficult to imagine a more comprehensive abandonment of rule-making authority and capacity.

Did UK officialdom see the point of the Lisbon Treaty?

In short, very important powers over the financial sector have been transferred from the UK state to EU institutions, as a result of the Lisbon Treaty and edicts from the European Commission arising from that treaty. The powers to authorize, to regulate and to supervise businesses are vital not just to those businesses and their shareholders, but also to their staff, to customers and to taxpayers. (After all, because profitable businesses pay tax, we all want to live in countries with many profitable companies.) Incredibly, it appears that UK officialdom may not have initially understood the implications of the Lisbon Treaty or appreciated the force of the subsequent "Communication".

An article in the *Financial Times* of 8th November 2011 speaks volumes.[15] In its words, describing an exchange which seems to have occurred a few weeks earlier,

> Sir Mervyn King [now Lord King] is not known as a man given to shouting. But during a meeting this summer in the genteel surroundings of London's Threadneedle Street, the Bank of England governor let fly. The visitor sitting across from him – a silver-haired Frenchman whose meticulous dress and proud demeanour appeared straight out of Gaullist central casting – was threatening to rein in the governor's new powers to set capital rules for Britain's banks. Sir Mervyn was having none of it. As his voice rose, his interpreter grew increasingly startled – particularly as the Frenchman refused to back down… The object of the governor's ire was Michel Barnier, the 60-year-old

---

13   Tim Ambler and Keith Boyfield *Financial Regulation: what is the best solution for the EU?* (London: Adam Smith Institute, 2009), p. 5.

14   On 4th June 2009 the Euronews agency interviewed the French finance minister, Christine Lagarde. The Euronews interviewer began by making a statement and then asking a question, "There is no absolute agreement in Europe on financial questions. What role does the Berlin-Paris relationship have?" Lagarde's reply was not to dispute that there was a special "Berlin Paris relationship". Instead she said, "Not all Europeans agree on everything at the same time. And the task for those Europeans convinced that they can play a real role on a regional level, is to manage to convince other partners. In this respect the Franco-German axis works well in staying firm on the matter of tax havens, rating agencies, speculative funds and European supervision. It's not really surprising that not everyone agrees because you have on one hand the members of the Eurozone and on the other those that are outside of the Eurozone. In particular there is Great Britain, which is directly concerned since it is a traditional hub of the financial services industry and it is not in the Eurozone." Statements along these lines, with clear hostility to the UK's financial services sector, have become more open and frequent in the last few years.

15   Alex Barker 'Barnier vs. the Brits', *Financial Times*, 8th November 2011.

former French foreign minister named two years ago as European internal market commissioner – a perch giving him oversight of the continent's financial industry. Arguably, no European Union job is of more consequence for the UK. That a stalwart from French president Nicolas Sarkozy's UMP party came to lord it over the City of London may one day go down as one of Britain's most important diplomatic failures in Brussels. After an initial British panic, relations with Mr Barnier were mostly marked by a tense but cordial truce… That detente, however, has collapsed.

It would be hard to imagine a more complete breakdown of the normal Anglo-French courtesies, but the point was that – in Barnier's eyes – the Lisbon Treaty had made it his job to regulate UK banks' capital standards. The matter was no longer contentious between Britain and France by themselves, as it might have been only 40 or 50 years ago, because the whole subject had been subsumed under a treaty that the governments of both nations had signed. That treaty in effect reduced both nations to the level of regions in one European super-state.

One well-informed observer of trends in financial regulation, Anthony Belchambers, chief executive of the London-based Futures and Options Association, commented in the same article in the *Financial Times* that, "Red tape, ill-informed tax initiatives, protectionist policies and high 'pass on' costs will damage the international reach of the City".[16] About 20 directives – on such matters as bank capital, transactions taxes and market infrastructure – were then in "the Brussels pipeline", as it has been termed. Their final implementation would fall not to British regulatory institutions, but to the EBA, the Paris-based ESMA and the Frankfurt-based EIOPA, all acting in coordination with the European Commission.

What, in more detail, have been the consequences so far?

EU intervention in the management of UK businesses

The prevention of artificial state subsidies has long been a central element in the process of European integration that began with the Treaty of Rome in 1957. Of course, if the government in one EU country extends financial aid to a particular business active in the EU-wide market, that business has an unfair advantage over similar businesses in other countries that do not have official support. In principle EU-wide competition law has, for many years, justified intervention by the Commission in the management of companies and industries. However, until the last decade or so the Commission had been reluctant to interfere in the UK financial sector, not least because the UK regarded itself as particularly proficient in the financial sphere and it had its own centres of apparent regulatory excellence in, for example, the Bank of England.

The UK's reputation was undermined by the Northern Rock affair from September 2007. A run on deposits gained such momentum that the Bank of England had to extend a large loan to Northern Rock, so that it still had enough cash to repay depositors. Although the loan was extended at a penalty rate, the European Commission determined that accompanying deposit guarantees constituted "state aid". [17] In its tendency to irritate and galvanize the bureaucracy in Brussels, the phrase "state aid" is like the proverbial red rag to a bull. On 18th March 2008 Neelie Kroes, the EU's Competition Commissioner, announced that Northern Rock would have to dismiss 2,000 of its 6,500 staff. This job destruction occurred in one of the UK's poorest regions. So, even before the Lisbon Treaty, the EU had acquired powers – through the EU-wide application of competition law – to intervene in the day-to-day operations of specific businesses.

At least in the Northern Rock case the impact of EU action was on a British organization that had requested central bank support and in that sense had failed. But much of British finance is profitable and has remained so in the last few difficult years. In City-based banks and other organizations profit streams can be large and volatile, and so also are the incomes of top staff. Incomes in the City of London often therefore have a major or even dominant bonus element, which helps the banks in handling the marked and unpredictable fluctuations in the profitability of different revenue streams. Here, too, the EU has decided to interfere. A new cap on top bankers' bonuses, to be limited to the same level as salary (or twice salary with explicit shareholder approval), is to take effect this year (i.e., in 2014).

The effects on the competitiveness of Britain's banking industry are undoubtedly adverse. The largest bank headquartered in the UK is HSBC, although most (about 80%) of its operations are outside the EU. Because it is UK-based, it has to apply the bonus cap to all its operations around the world, a development about which

---

[16]   The quotation is also from the Alex Barker article on Barnier in the *Financial Times* on 8th November 2011.

[17]   See pp. 10 – 11 of my 2008 pamphlet *Northern Rock and the European Union* (London: Global Vision).

it has been openly angry and hostile. Of course, one way of side-stepping the new EU regulation would be to relocate the headquarters from London to, for example, Hong Kong, where in fact the bulk of the profit is earned.[18] As Norman Lamont, a former Chancellor of the Exchequer, remarked in an article in *The Daily Telegraph* on 26th February 2013, government interventions in pay create "distortions, as companies find ways of circumventing them. If implemented, the new pay restrictions would lead to an exodus of bankers and traders to Switzerland and the Far East."[19] (Nowadays opinion surveys routinely find that such Asian city states as Hong Kong and Singapore have a more business-friendly and light-regulation environment than EU nations. Hong Kong and Singapore also have economies more heavily reliant on international business services than the UK, and in that respect face the same challenges in the 21st century as the UK. When Hong Kong returned to Chinese control in 1997, its income per head – as measured by the International Monetary Fund and on a so-called "purchasing power parity" basis in terms of current dollars [i.e., dollars of the year in question] – was much the same as in the UK, with Singapore somewhat higher. Chart 6 shows that in the last 15 years they have both moved far ahead of the UK.)

Compared with banking, insurance has been out of the media limelight in the last few years. Unlike bankers, top insurance underwriters and brokers have not been blamed for the Great Recession of late 2008 and 2009. However, the UK's insurance industry also has been affected by EU regulation. Lloyd's of London, which dates its origins back to 1688, remains the focal point for the UK's international insurance industry. Its four largest national markets (by premium written) are the USA, the UK, Canada and Australia, while the EU is something of a side-show. (Premiums from the USA are 20 times those from France.) But Lloyd's' global outlook has not exempted it from the EU's regulations. Because it is located in the EU, it must comply with them whether it likes to or not.

Since 2009 these have taken the form of the introduction, the aborted introduction and then the re-introduction of a capital regime known as "Solvency II". UK insurers have spent billions of pounds – in management time, consultancy fees and the like – so that their businesses can meet the Solvency II standards. Unfortunately, German and French insurance companies were for some years at loggerheads over the provisions of Solvency II, and could not reach agreement. So much of the money committed to Solvency II by Lloyd's of London and other UK insurance companies was spent prematurely and, to that extent, wasted. Andrew Bailey, a top Bank of England

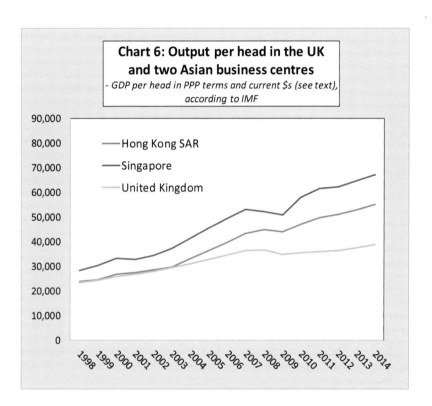

Chart 6: Output per head in the UK and two Asian business centres
- GDP per head in PPP terms and current $s (see text), according to IMF

official, said in February 2013 that the "mounting costs" of Solvency II implementation were "frankly indefensible".[20] Some insurance companies have become so irritated by the delays and inefficiency of EU regulation that they have left London altogether.[21] Happily, at the time of writing (May 2014) the French and the Germans seem to have patched up their differences, and the implementation date for Solvency II is now widely expected to be January 2016. (But that date has not been finalized and it could still be shifted.)

---

[18]   On 24th April 2014 HSBC put its global headquarters building, in Canary Wharf, London, up for sale. HSBC has denied that it intends to change the location of its fiscal and regulatory headquarters from London.

[19]   Norman Lamont 'A cap on bankers' bonuses would be lunacy', *The Daily Telegraph*, 26th February 2013.

[20]   Alistair Gray 'Lloyd's chief airs Solvency II frustration', *Financial Times*, 27th March 2013.

[21]   Alistair Gray 'Lloyd's insurer off to Bermuda', *Financial Times*, 26th April 2013.

The EU spreads the tax net: the Financial Transactions Tax

European governments have generally been averse to giving up their powers to tax and spend. They have not handed over such powers to EU institutions. Their retention of key fiscal prerogatives goes some way to explaining why EU institutions have tried to boost their power by instead grabbing "competences", and multiplying directives and regulations. Nevertheless, the administrative basis for the collection of value added tax has been subject to the jurisdiction of the EU since 1993. (Indeed, it was subject to that of the European Economic Community [the EU's predecessor, which – as noted above – was once known in British debate as "the Common Market"] from the 1960s.)

The Great Recession has been widely blamed on the alleged iniquities of free-market capitalism and, particularly, on the supposed greed and myopia of its financial institutions. One sequel across the EU was for governments to demand that extra taxes be imposed on the financial sector, with the revenue perhaps to be credited – like a proportion of VAT receipts – to EU institutions. The European Commission was alert to this discussion, and published a range of documents and statements about a new "Financial Transactions Tax", also labelled, for public relations purposes, "the Robin Hood tax". The Commission undoubtedly wanted the tax to go ahead. To an uninformed observer, the tax rates (of 0.1% on securities and 0.01% on derivatives) were very low and therefore innocuous. However, the City of London specializes in highly competitive areas of financial trade, mostly between big firms and of a so-called "wholesale" nature, with very narrow margins between buying and selling prices. The 0.1% and 0.01% tax rates were higher than the profit margins in some kinds of financial transaction, which would therefore become uneconomic and would either leave the EU or cease. On 14th February 2013 the European Commission put its name on a Powerpoint presentation that unashamedly envisaged a 75% fall in derivatives trading.[22] It was plainly indifferent to the job losses (running into tens of thousands) and ruined livelihoods that would result. Its officials must have been aware – indeed, they may have privately been delighted – that the job losses and ruined livelihoods would be mostly in London and the South-east of England.

The British government has been supine in many of its dealings with the European Commission and other EU member states. But, from the early days of the proposals, it viewed the FTT as misguided and potentially leading to an unjustified extension of EU power. It became clear that, even if the UK itself did not adopt the tax on transactions between UK citizens (or between UK citizens and those in the rest of the world), the UK would still have to levy the tax on transactions involving EU-originated and euro-denominated securities and derivatives. In other words, the FTT would not respect national boundaries and would in effect be "extra-territorial". (In qualification, the details are complex and uncertain, as the precise administrative format of the FTT has not yet been agreed.)

As remarked by the Washington-based Investment Companies Institute, "The financial transaction tax (FTT) being considered by several European countries would have an extraordinary extra-territorial effect. The tax would crash across borders. All investors would be hit."[23] The British government therefore took the Commission to the European Court of Justice to determine the legality of the FTT and its extra-territorial features. At the end of April 2014 the ECJ threw out the British government's case, on the grounds that it was premature while details of the FTT's structure had not been decided. While appearing to leave the matter open, the truth is that the ECJ virtually always decides such disputes in favour of the enlargement of EU power. There can be little doubt that the hope of the European Commission, and indeed of virtually EU governments apart from the British, is that a FTT will ultimately be collected across the EU, including the UK, just as VAT is collected across the EU at present. Because the financial services industries are much larger relative to national output in the UK, the UK would of course be a major loser. (The talk is of over £3billion of FTT revenues being levied in the UK and paid to EU institutions, just as a proportion of VAT revenue is paid at present).

Estimates of the damage to the UK are bound to be debatable, perhaps even rather precarious, until the FTT proposals have become more definite. But it is worth mentioning one point of view, from Sam Bowman, Head of Research at the Adam Smith Institute, in a November 2011 release based on a report it had commissioned. In his view, the FTT would cause "huge damage" to the UK. To quote, "It would wipe out London's derivatives sector, destroying jobs and driving other traders overseas. By destroying a critical part of Britain's most lucrative industry, an EU Financial Transaction Tax would be killing the goose that lays the golden eggs. The EU is proposing this tax to distract from the real culprits for Europe's troubles – spendthrift

---

[22]   *Implementing enhanced cooperation in the area of the Financial Transaction Tax* (Brussels: European Commission, 2013), slide 20 of the Powerpoint presentation.

[23]   Keith Lawson, 'The extraordinarily extraterritorial proposal to tax global financial transactions', posted on the website of the Investment Companies Institute, 10th April, 2013. (See www.ici.org.)

governments who cannot balance their books. Using markets as a scapegoat might buy Eurozone leaders some political credibility, but it would ruin the City of London."[24]

The costs of the AIFMD

In the original 2009 version of this essay I identified the Alternative Investment Fund Management Directive (or AIFMD) as an immediate threat to the efficiency of the UK financial services sector. At that stage the AIFMD was only a proposal, but its contents were unlikely to change all that much and in the end they have not done so. The AIFMD was intended as a means of disciplining the "alternative fund management industry", particularly private equity and so-called "hedge funds". (Hedge funds pursue a range of investment strategies, sometimes taking on more risk than conventional fund managers subject to a benchmark.) In some European countries private equity investment and the hedge fund industry were seen as being emblematic of cutthroat Anglo-American capitalism. Specifically, their borrowings were criticized as being risky and excessive, and as being particularly to blame for the Great Recession.

The AIFMD therefore introduced restrictions on the degree of leverage, as well as imposing an assortment of rules about business conduct, reporting arrangements, provisions for collateral, asset registration and so on. The new rules applied, for example, to UK investment trusts, which in some cases had been in existence for over a hundred years and had magnificent long-run investment returns. The directive was interventionist and prescriptive, and undoubtedly added to costs. It took effect in July 2013, although with minor delays in some countries.

A year earlier the accountancy firm, Deloittes, had prepared a report on the industry's reaction. Industry respondents characterised the AIFMD as "protectionist", in that it could be interpreted as "a building block of 'Fortress Europe'". The explanation was that the business conduct rules were burdensome, so that 68% of respondents believed that the directive would lead to less non-EU managers operating in the EU. The same proportion, 68%, also thought that the AIFMD's compliance burden would reduce the competitiveness of the EU's alternative investment funds industry.

---

[24]   'EU Financial Transaction Tax would wipe out derivatives markets and cost UK £25.5bn', release from London's Adam Smith Institute, 4th November 2011.

A particular grievance was the burden of new "depositary costs". In the report's words, "Many managers will need to appoint a depositary for the first time and will face additional fees from depositaries for the safekeeping and oversight of assets falling under the strict and potentially expensive liability provisions. 84% of respondents are significantly concerned about the depositary costs that they will incur as a result of AIFMD."

Even the European Central Bank said that the directive goes too far. Of course highly leveraged businesses can be a menace to the stability of the banking industry. Nevertheless, the restrictions in the directive were widely viewed as disproportionate to the risks posed to the banking system by the alternative investment industry. Since most alternative investment management companies in the EU were and continue to be based in London, many observers suspected that the motivation – coming from the French and being channelled via the Commission – was pure beggar-thy-neighbour, to undermine a significant source of value added in the UK's capital city.

What can we do?

The British stumbled into the creation of the world's largest empire, and spread their language, their law and their culture across the globe. That remains their most spectacular achievement as a nation. Because of this achievement, our country is ideally equipped to become the provider of high-value-added services to businesses across the globe and for us to be "the gaffers" of the world economy. The notion of "a national strategy" is problematic and controversial, because ultimately in a free society individuals must decide what is in their best interests. Nevertheless, a reasonable surmise is that people in Britain would be well-advised to let other countries concentrate on low-value-added mass production of basic products and manufactured goods. In the 21st century a sensible choice for talented and capable people in our country is to specialise on complex service activities that demand knowledge, responsibility, judgement and individual flair, and we should sell our skills in these areas to the world as a whole. The world market for such services will undoubtedly become increasingly important relative to the European market as the century progresses. Over time the world market for international business services will become a multiple of the European market.

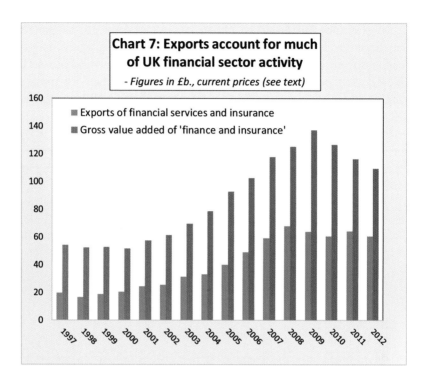

Chart 7: Exports account for much of UK financial sector activity
- Figures in £b., current prices (see text)

In a 2009 interview in *Prospect* magazine Adair Turner, the then chairman of the Financial Services Authority, remarked that much financial services activity is "socially useless".[25] He implied that the UK could see much of its financial services sector contract without any loss to the wider economy and society. That was nonsense. As has been shown here, the bulk of the value added in London-based financial services is sold to the rest of the world. Production of these services therefore pays - £ for £, $ for $ and € for € – for our imports. If our exports of financial services were to fall, we would either have to import less or to export more of other goods and services. Those other exports would of course have a resource cost. Turner's contention that UK financial services are in some sense "too large" is quite wrong. Of course, exports of £50 billion - £60 billion are very big for the UK, since the UK's GDP is about £1,700 billion. Yet we account for little more than 3% of world GDP. The UK specialist, wholesale financial services sector may be more than 3% of the UK's GDP, but it is roughly 0.1% of world output. In a global context the notion that these services are disproportionately large is preposterous. (Chart 7 compares exports of financial services and insurance, according to the official *Pink Book* published by the Office for National Statistics, with gross value added in finance and insurance, according to the *Blue Book*, also from the ONS. In 2012 exports were £60.4 billion, compared with Gross Value Added of £109.5 billion. Of course most of the financial sector's domestic output – that is, output for UK customers – is located outside London. Hence, the above statement, "the bulk of the value added in London-based financial services is sold to the rest of the world".)

In this essay I have shown that Britain's pattern of specialisation in the last 30 years has been towards the supply of business services to other countries. Our exports of international business services – and particularly of financial services – have boomed. But it is vital in these areas – where so much depends on laws and regulations, and their fair interpretation – that our government is able to propose and endorse rules and regulations that it likes, and to oppose and repudiate those that it dislikes. The more that law-making and the enforcement of regulations passes to Brussels, Frankfurt, Paris and Luxembourg, the less will the UK be able to defend its interests.

As this essay has shown, many examples of EU interventions in our economy have directly harmed people's businesses and livelihoods. It is naïve to imagine that the volume and intensity of these interventions will decline in coming years. On the contrary, the centralizing and interventionist impulses in the EU are remorseless. As Lord Denning remarked over 20 years ago, "Our sovereignty has been taken away by the European Court of Justice… No longer is European law an income tide flowing up the estuaries of England. It is now like a tidal wave bringing down our sea walls and flowing inland over our fields and houses – to the dismay of all."[26]

If we remain in the European Union on the present terms, it will become increasingly difficult for Britain to further its role as the world's leading centre for international business services. International financial services – in which the UK excelled in the two decades to 2008 – are already in retreat and remain particularly at risk. Our government's ability to mould a favourable regulatory environment, or even a neutral regulatory environment, has been undermined by our acceptance of the Lisbon Treaty. The prosperity of London's key industries will become yet more vulnerable to the whims of legislators and regulators from other countries.

---

[25]   Adair Turner roundtable 'How to tame global finance', pp. 34 – 8, *Prospect*, September 2009.

[26]   Lord Denning *Introduction to the European Court of Justice: Judges or Policy Makers?* (London: Bruges Group, 1990).

Bluntly, key policy-making individuals in Germany, France and other continental European countries have long disliked the financial services industry, and resented the UK's past success in these activities. The euro was seen as a means of shifting Europe's financial centre of gravity from London to the European mainland. In the words of Wolfgang Munchau, a prominent columnist on the *Financial Times*, "...if the Eurozone has a collective interest in anything, it is to stop the City acting as its main financial centre."[27] But that does not go far enough. Prominent European politicians hardly bother to hide their aversion to financial activity or their desire to handicap or even expel the most complex and highly-paid financial industries from the EU. While the UK remains a member of the EU, expulsion from the EU means expulsion from the UK.

The 2009 edition of this publication forecast that the Lisbon Treaty would lead to a shift in regulation from the UK to the EU, and this shift would imply extra costs, tighter controls and reduced competitiveness for the UK's financial services sector. That forecast has been correct. Until quite recently the financial services sector, with its exports growing at a double-digit annual % rate for over 20 years, was the UK's most successful set of industries. The move to EU regulation has stopped that growth. It has therefore, directly and measurably, reduced the prosperity of our nation. If the British government is to recover the power to set the financial sector's rules, a greater degree of regulatory autonomy from Brussels (and indeed from Frankfurt, Paris and Luxembourg as well) must be sought. This is one reason, although only one reason, why a radical re-appraisal of EU membership has become essential.

---

[27]   Wolfgang Munchau 'The bonus issue is the first shot in a long battle', *Financial Times*, 4th March 2013.